Juvenile

Y0-CAY-975

GAYLORD

# Hair

By Cynthia Klingel and Robert B. Noyed

Reading consultant: Cecilia Minden-Cupp, Ph.D.,
Adjunct Professor, College of Continuing and Professional Studies, University of Virginia

Gareth Stevens
Publishing

Please visit our Web site www.garethstevens.com. For a free color catalog of all our high-quality books, call toll free 1-800-542-2595 or fax 1-877-542-2596.

Library of Congress Cataloging-in-Publication Data

Kligel, Cynthia.
   Hair / by Cynthia Klingel and Robert B. Noyed. |
      p. cm. - (Let's read about our bodies)
   Includes bibliographical references and index.
   Summary: A simple introduction to hair, its characteristics, and how to take care of it.
   ISBN: 978-1-4339-3362-2 (lib. bdg.)
   ISBN: 978-1-4339-3363-9 (pbk.)
   ISBN: 978-1-4339-3364-6 (6-pack)
   1. Hair–Juvenile literature.   [1. Hair.]   I. Noyed, Robert B.   II. Title.
   QP88.3.K555   2002
   611.78–dc21                                        20010550056

New edition published 2010 by
**Gareth Stevens Publishing**
111 East 14th Street, Suite 349
New York, NY 10003

New text and images this edition copyright © 2010 Gareth Stevens Publishing

Original edition published 2003 by Weekly Reader® Books
An imprint of Gareth Stevens Publishing
Original edition text and images copyright © 2003 Gareth Stevens Publishing

Art direction: Haley Harasymiw, Tammy Gruenewald
Page layout: Daniel Hosek, Katherine A. Goedheer
Editorial direction: Kerri O'Donnell, Diane Laska Swanke

Photo credits: Cover, p. 9 shutterstock.com; pp. 5, 7, 11, 13, 15, 17, 19, 21 Gregg Andersen.

Printed in the United States of America

CPSIA compliance information: Batch #WW10GS: For further information contact Gareth Stevens, New York, New York at 1-800-542-2595.

# Table of Contents

**Boldface** words appear in the glossary.

# All About Hair

This is my hair.
My hair is on
my head.

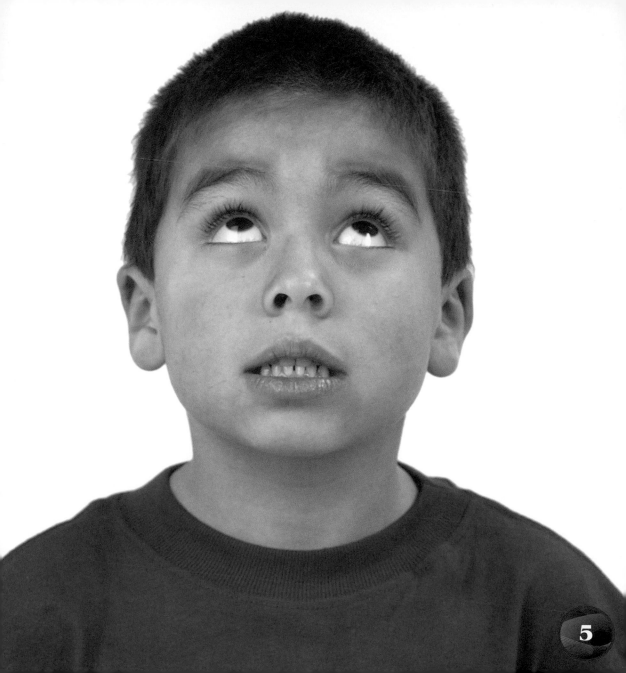

Hair can be many colors. What color is your hair?

Hair can be long or short.

Some hair is **curly**.
Some hair is not.

Sometimes I get my hair cut.

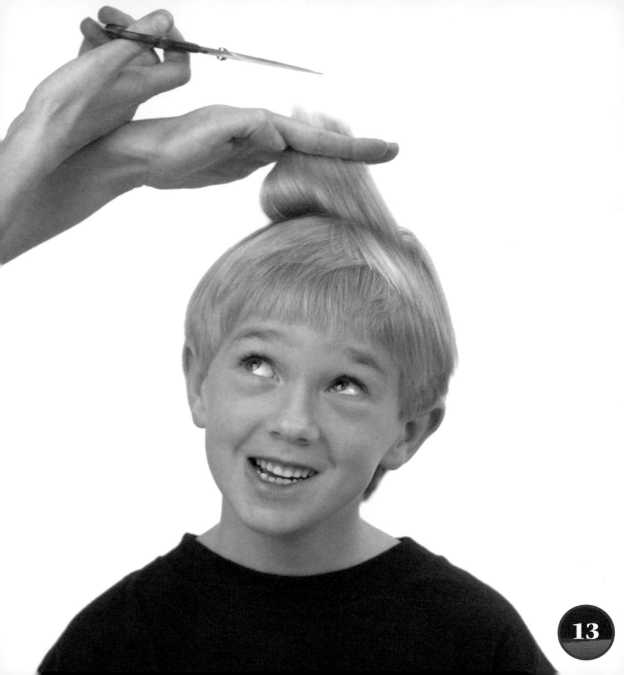

# Hair Care

I keep my hair **neat**. I use a brush and **comb**.

Sometimes I wear things in my hair.

I keep my hair **clean**. I wash it with **shampoo** and water.

I can have fun
with my hair!

# Glossary

**clean:** to be free from dirt

**comb:** a flat tool with a row of teeth used to make your hair neat

**curly:** bending or twisting in a spiral shape

**neat:** clean and orderly

**shampoo:** a liquid soap used to wash hair

# For More Information

## Books

Johnson, Dinah. *Hair Dance!* New York: Henry Holt, 2007.

Munsch, Robert. *Aaron's Hair*. New York: Scholastic, 2002.

Saltzberg, Barney. *Crazy Hair Day*. Somerville, MA: Candlewick, 2008.

Watt, Fiona. *The Usborne Book of Hair Braiding*. Evelith, MN: Usborne Books, 2005.

## Web Sites

**Your Hair**

*kidshealth.org/kid/htbw/hair.html*

For more information about your hair

# Index

## About the Authors

**Cynthia Klingel** has worked as a high school English teacher and an elementary school teacher. She is currently the curriculum director for a Minnesota school district. Cynthia Klingel lives with her family in Mankato, Minnesota.

**Robert B. Noyed** started his career as a newspaper reporter. Since then, he has worked in school communications and public relations at the state and national level. Robert B. Noyed lives with his family in Brooklyn Center, Minnesota.